CYPRUS 2016 HUMAN RIGHTS REPORT

Since 1974 the southern part of Cyprus has been under the control of the government of the Republic of Cyprus, while the northern part, administered by Turkish Cypriots, proclaimed itself the "Turkish Republic of Northern Cyprus" ("TRNC") in 1983. The United States does not recognize the "TRNC," nor does any country other than Turkey. A substantial number of Turkish troops remained on the island. A buffer zone, or "Green Line," patrolled by the UN Peacekeeping Force in Cyprus (UNFICYP), separates the two sides.

REPUBLIC OF CYPRUS

EXECUTIVE SUMMARY

The Republic of Cyprus is a constitutional republic and multiparty presidential democracy. In 2013 voters elected President Nicos Anastasiades in free and fair elections. On May 22, voters elected 56 representatives to the 80-seat House of Representatives (Vouli Antiprosopon) in free and fair elections.

Civilian authorities maintained effective control over the security forces.

The most significant problems during the year remained trafficking in persons for sexual exploitation and labor; police abuse and their degrading treatment of persons in custody and asylum seekers; and violence against women, including spousal abuse.

Other problems during the year included: prison overcrowding; lack of separation of pretrial detainees from convicted criminals; prolonged detention of asylum seekers and irregular migrants in prison-like conditions; deportation of rejected asylum seekers before they had an opportunity to appeal their asylum decision; lack of full access to and administration of some religious sites; government corruption; incidents of violence against children; instances of discrimination and violence against members of minority ethnic and national groups; and societal discrimination against lesbian, gay, bisexual, transgender, and intersex (LGBTI) persons.

The government investigated and prosecuted corruption and officials who committed violations.

Section 1. Respect for the Integrity of the Person, Including Freedom from:

a. Arbitrary Deprivation of Life and other Unlawful or Politically Motivated Killings

There were no reports that the government or its agents committed arbitrary or unlawful killings.

b. Disappearance

There were no reports of politically motivated disappearances.

c. Torture and Other Cruel, Inhuman, or Degrading Treatment or Punishment

The constitution and law prohibit such practices. There were reports, however, that police engaged in abusive tactics and degrading treatment of suspects. For example, on April 24, the NGO Action for Equality, Support, and Antiracism (KISA) released a video showing a female police officer at Mennoyia Detention Center for irregular migrants repeatedly swearing at detainees, one of whom was recording the scene, and insulting a Muslim detainee's religion and his mother. A few days earlier, the detainees had protested their detention conditions. According to a July 14 police statement, the female officer was suspended from duty and police opened a criminal and disciplinary investigation against her. After the conclusion of the investigation, her suspension was lifted, and she returned to work at a different police station while the criminal prosecution and disciplinary procedure against her are pending. The ombudsman found the incident to be a grave breach of the detainee's human rights that amounted to degrading treatment.

During the year the ombudsman, who also acts as the country's national preventive mechanism under the Optional Protocol to the UN Convention against Torture, received several complaints of mistreatment, discriminatory, and degrading behavior, including complaints of verbal, physical, and sexual abuse, from inmates in the Central Prison and in detention centers. The ombudsman was also examining a report that police abused a detainee during a deportation procedure.

In June the ombudsman issued a report drawing attention to statements of certain police officials who had publicly praised their colleagues for subjecting detainees to violence. For example, after the conviction of two police officers for beating a detainee in Polis police station, the station chief described their actions as bravery and the detainee as a "drug addict and psychopath who sends police officers to prison."

Prison and Detention Center Conditions

Despite some improvement, prison and detention center conditions, including detention centers for asylum seekers and undocumented migrants pending deportation, did not sufficiently meet international standards, and prison overcrowding was a problem.

Physical Conditions: Overcrowding continued to be a problem for Nicosia Central Prison, the only prison in the Republic of Cyprus, but to a lesser extent than in previous years. The prison's official capacity was increased to 528 from 469 inmates; the maximum number of inmates held during the year was 653. The ombudsman reported a further but not substantial decrease in the number of prisoners due to the concerted effort of the prison's new management. None of the major complaints submitted to the ombudsman were related to overcrowding.

Prison authorities held juvenile pretrial detainees in cells separate from convicted juveniles, but the two groups shared the same grounds in their daily activities.

The ombudsman reported improvement in prison and detention center conditions and treatment of prisoners and detainees after several visits to facilities during the year. The ombudsman reported the reduction in the number of migrant detainees in detention centers was a result of the policy instituted last year to transfer them to Mennoyia within 48 hours. The ombudsman also reported improvements in the detention facilities of several police stations. Prison authorities reported that prisoners were separated by health condition but overcrowding prevented separate detention space for drug users. Long-term and short-term prisoners were not held separately, as prison policy for separation of prisoners was based on their individual needs, the risks involved, and their behavior, and not the duration of their sentence. Prisoners serving a life sentence have a cell of their own.

Authorities reportedly held migrants detained on deportation orders in nearly all police stations together with detainees charged with criminal offenses.

Approximately 45 percent of prisoners in the Central Prison were non-Cypriots convicted for criminal offenses. One-third of non-Cypriots were convicted for immigration-related offenses, such as illegal employment and possession of false documents for entering the country.

In its annual report for 2014-15, Amnesty International criticized the routine detention of hundreds of migrants and certain categories of asylum seekers in "cramped, prison-like conditions" at the Mennoyia Detention Center, the country's main migrant detention facility, pending deportation. According to the report, detainees complained about the limited time allowed for outdoor exercise, food quality, and having their cells locked at night.

The ombudsman reported considerable reduction of detainees at Mennoyia during the year. The ombudsman reported that most of the complaints received from Mennoyia detainees during the year were related to migration issues, not to detention conditions or mistreatment. The ombudsman, however, commented that migrants and asylum seekers continued to be detained for deportation purposes for periods longer than the stated government policy, although there was no prospect they would be deported. A considerable number of detainees at Mennoyia Detention Center were awaiting a decision on their request for international protection or for adjudication of their appeals against the rejection of their asylum applications. In some cases, detainees were deported before final adjudication of their asylum applications. The ombudsman intervened and prevented some of the deportations. In a February report, the ombudsman again warned authorities that deportation of asylum seekers while court proceedings were still pending could amount to violation of the principle of nonrefoulement, which could bring into question the legality of the deportation order and detention.

Administration: While prisoners in the Central Prison had access to a church and mosque, detention centers did not have facilities for religious observance.

Independent Monitoring: The government permitted prison visits by independent human rights observers, and such visits, unrestricted and unannounced, occurred during the year. The Ombudsman's Office, in its capacity as the national preventive mechanism, and the prison board visited the Central Prison on a regular basis. The House of Representatives Committee on Equal Opportunities for Men and Women, the commissioner for children's rights, and the commissioner for the protection of personal data also visited the prison.

The NGO KISA reported that police sometimes used violence to suppress detainees' protests in Mennoyia Detention Center and that the government continued the policy of detaining migrants while their appeals against the rejection of their asylum applications were still pending. Following a January 25 to 29 visit to the country, the UN Subcommittee on the Prevention of Torture stated that, while the country had made many improvements concerning treatment of those in detention, it still faced several problems, particularly regarding the independent monitoring of places of detention and the treatment of migrants.

d. Arbitrary Arrest or Detention

The law prohibits arbitrary arrest and detention, and the government generally observed these prohibitions.

Role of the Police and Security Apparatus

Police enforce the law and combat criminal activity. The Cyprus National Guard, backed by a contingent of Greek military forces, the Hellenic Force in Cyprus, protects national security. The National Guard reports to the Ministry of Defense, which reports to the president, while police report to the Ministry of Justice and Public Order. The president appoints the chief of police.

The Independent Authority for the Investigation of Allegations and Complaints against Police is an independent committee appointed by the Council of Ministers to investigate alleged human rights abuses by police. The body also has authority to investigate complaints of police bribery, corruption, unlawful financial gain, abuse of power, preferential treatment, and conduct unbecoming a police officer. The Independent Authority appointed independent investigators from a list submitted by the attorney general to look into complaints. The authority functioned appropriately and its investigations resulted in the criminal prosecution of 12 police officers in 2014, the most recent year for which statistics were available.

On June 23, a police officer and his wife were shot and killed and a second officer was seriously injured in a mafia-style shooting while dining at an Ayia Napa tourist resort restaurant with a local businessman rumored to be a major crime lord, who was also killed in the attack. On August 9, the attorney general appointed three criminal prosecutors to investigate possible police corruption in relation to the case. From January to September, the attorney general ordered criminal investigations against 11 police officers.

During the year 212 prison officers participated in seminars and educational courses in the country and abroad on human rights issues, women's education, employability of youths, prevention of mistreatment, diversity, treatment of detainees, terrorism, electronic monitoring, sexual harassment in the workplace, effective negotiations, and other subjects.

Arrest Procedures and Treatment of Detainees

The law requires judicially issued arrest warrants, and authorities respected this requirement. Authorities may not detain a person for more than one day without referral of the case to a court for extension of detention. Most periods of investigative detention did not exceed 10 days before the filing of formal charges. Detainees were promptly informed of the charges against them, and the charges were presented in a language they could understand. The attorney general made efforts to minimize pretrial detention, especially in cases of serious crimes.

While attorneys generally had access to detainees, the Council of Europe's Committee for the Prevention of Torture (CPT) noted in a 2014 report that persons apprehended by police were usually able to speak in private with an ex officio lawyer only at the time of their first court appearance. In criminal cases the state provides indigent detainees with an attorney. To qualify for free legal aid, however, detainees require a court decision, based on their financial need, before a lawyer is assigned. In its report, the CPT noted this system inevitably delayed detainees' access to a lawyer.

There is a system of bail. The government claimed the right to deport foreign nationals for reasons of public interest, regardless of whether criminal charges had been filed against them or they had been convicted of a crime. Trial delays were common and partially caused by lengthy legal procedures, which caused a larger workload for the courts.

Detainees' Ability to Challenge Lawfulness of Detention before a Court: Detainees have the right to appeal to the Supreme Court to challenge the legal basis and length of their detention or for a writ of habeas corpus. If the application is successful, authorities should immediately release the detainee. NGOs reported a number of cases, however, of asylum seekers and irregular migrants who successfully challenged their detention before the Supreme Court, but the administration immediately issued new detention orders and rearrested them.

Protracted Detention of Rejected Asylum Seekers or Stateless Persons: According to Amnesty International, authorities routinely detained hundreds of migrants and certain categories of asylum seekers in prison-like conditions for extended periods while awaiting deportation. Detainees reportedly included unaccompanied minors.

While the government's policy was not to hold such persons in detention for long periods and to release them and provide them residency permits if they were not deported within 18 months, there were reports that migrants and asylum seekers were held beyond 18 months or, if released, were rearrested and incarcerated on different grounds. In a March 31 report following his December 2015 visit, the Council of Europe's commissioner for human rights expressed concern over the wide use of migrant detention, often for excessively long periods, and the practice of rearresting and redetaining migrants. The commissioner urged the government to end the practice of migrant detention, especially of asylum seekers and migrants deprived of liberty when there was no reasonable prospect of their deportation.

The ombudsman received a number of complaints concerning detainees held for considerable time, based on deportation orders. The ombudsman repeatedly called on the government not to detain foreigners for deportation when there was no prospect of deportation because they did not have travel documents. In April an NGO reported that authorities rearrested on different charges rejected asylum seekers whose appeals against the rejection of their applications were still pending before the court.

An NGO reported that a number of undocumented foreigners arrested for illegal stays in the country remained in long-term detention.

e. Denial of Fair Public Trial

The law and constitution provide for an independent judiciary, and the government generally respected judicial independence.

Trial Procedures

The law provides for the right to a fair public trial, and an independent judiciary generally enforced this right. Officials informed defendants promptly and in detail of the charges against them. The constitution provides for fair and public trials without undue delay, and defendants have the right to be present and to consult with an attorney in a timely manner. Authorities provided an attorney for defendants who could not afford one, and defendants were allowed adequate time and facilities to prepare a defense. Authorities provided free interpretation as necessary through all stages of the trial; defendants have access to government-held evidence and have the right to confront prosecution or plaintiff witnesses and present evidence or witnesses on their behalf. The law also provides that defendants and their attorneys have access to government-held evidence related to their cases. Defendants enjoy a presumption of innocence and have a right of appeal. The government generally respected the above rights and provided them to all defendants.

Political Prisoners and Detainees

There were no reports of political prisoners or detainees.

Civil Judicial Procedures and Remedies

There is an independent and impartial judiciary in civil matters, permitting claimants to bring lawsuits seeking damages for or cessation of human rights violations, and citizens used this procedure. Individuals could appeal cases involving alleged human rights violations by the state to the European Court of Human Rights (ECHR) once they exhausted all avenues of appeal in domestic courts.

Property Restitution

According to the law, the minister of interior is the guardian of the properties of Turkish Cypriots who have not had permanent residence in the government-controlled area since 1974. Ownership remains with the original owner, but the sale or transfer of Turkish Cypriot property under the guardianship of the minister requires the approval of the government. The minister has the authority to return properties to Turkish Cypriot applicants after examining the circumstances of each case. Owners can appeal the minister's decisions to the Supreme Court.

During the year Turkish Cypriots filed seven court cases seeking to reclaim property located in the government-controlled area, including two filed with the Supreme Court. Of the Supreme Court cases, one application challenging the Ministry of Interior's decision to block the sale of properties was dismissed on procedural grounds. The other Supreme Court application requesting exemption of property from the guardianship law was also rejected on procedural grounds. In one of the civil cases, the district court found in favor of the plaintiff and ordered the government to pay 79,243 euros ($87,200) plus interest in compensation for lost rent and nonpecuniary damages. In the other civil cases, the courts found in favor of the government.

The ombudsman, using her oversight authority on matters of alleged racism and discrimination, examined several complaints of delays in the examination of claims involving Turkish Cypriot properties in the government-controlled area. Authorities approved or expedited the examination of some of the claims after the ombudsman's intervention.

f. Arbitrary or Unlawful Interference with Privacy, Family, Home, or Correspondence

The law prohibits such actions, and there were no reports that the government failed to respect these prohibitions.

Section 2. Respect for Civil Liberties, Including:

a. Freedom of Speech and Press

The law provides for freedom of speech and press, and the government generally respected these rights. An independent press, an effective judiciary, and a functioning democratic political system combined to promote freedom of speech and press.

Freedom of Speech and Expression: The law criminalizes incitement to hatred and violence against anyone based on race, color, religion, genealogical origin, national or ethnic origin, or sexual orientation. Such acts are punishable by up to five years' imprisonment, a fine of up to 10,000 euros ($11,000), or both. In 2015 police examined 11 complaints of verbal assault and/or hate speech based on ethnic origin, religion, sexual orientation, and color. Authorities opened criminal prosecutions in three cases. One case resulted in a conviction, and two were pending trial.

Press and Media Freedoms: The law penalizes the use of geographical names and toponyms in the country other than those included in the gazetteer the government presented at the 1987 Fifth UN Conference on the Standardization of Geographical Names. According to the law, anyone who publishes, imports, distributes, or sells maps, books, or any other documents in print or digital form that contain geographical names and toponyms on the island of Cyprus other than those permitted, commits an offense punishable by up to three years in prison, a fine of up to 50,000 euros ($55,000), or both.

In February the mayor of Myrtou village and the leader of the Green party submitted to the Permanent Cypriot Committee for the Standardization of Geographical Names a complaint against the Bicommunal Technical Committee on Cultural Heritage (one of the bicommunal working groups set up as part of the UN-facilitated peace talks) for using in a January publication the name Turkish Cypriot authorities gave Myrtou post-1974. The complaint was before the attorney general for a legal opinion.

Internet Freedom

The government did not restrict or disrupt access to the internet or censor online content, and there were no credible reports that the government monitored private online communications without appropriate legal authority. According to statistics compiled by Eurostat, approximately 71 percent of the population used the internet in 2015.

The law criminalizes the use of computer systems to incite and promote prejudice, hatred, or violence. Such acts are punishable by up to five years' imprisonment, a fine of up to 35,000 euros ($38,500), or both.

Academic Freedom and Cultural Events

There were generally no government restrictions on academic freedom or cultural events.

b. Freedom of Peaceful Assembly and Association

The law and constitution provide for the freedoms of assembly and association, and the government generally respected these rights.

c. Freedom of Religion

See the Department of State's *International Religious Freedom Report* at www.state.gov/religiousfreedomreport/.

d. Freedom of Movement, Internally Displaced Persons, Protection of Refugees, and Stateless Persons

The law provides for freedom of movement within government-controlled areas, foreign travel, emigration, and repatriation, and the government generally respected these rights.

Abuse of Migrants, Refugees, and Stateless Persons: NGOs and the Ombudsman's Office, in its capacity as the national preventive mechanism (NPM), reported that some rejected asylum seekers under detention submitted complaints of psychological and verbal abuse by police officers at Mennoyia detention center. In January the UN Subcommittee on Prevention of Torture and other Cruel, Inhuman or Degrading Treatment or Punishment undertook an advisory visit to the country to provide technical advice and assistance to the NPM. Foreign nationals sentenced to a few months' imprisonment for entering the country illegally were generally deported as soon as their travel documents were ready.

The government cooperated with the Office of the UN High Commissioner for Refugees (UNHCR) and other humanitarian organizations in providing protection and assistance to internally displaced persons (IDPs), refugees, returning refugees, asylum seekers, stateless persons, and other persons of concern, including migrants.

In-country Movement: The government did not restrict Greek Cypriots from traveling to the area administered by Turkish Cypriots, but it generally advised them against spending the night at Greek Cypriot properties occupied by Turkish Cypriots or Turks, gambling in the area administered by Turkish Cypriots, or buying or developing property there. NGOs reported that the government prohibits recognized non-Cypriot refugees with temporary residence status and asylum seekers from crossing to the area administered by the Turkish Cypriots, asserting it could not assure their safety in an area not under its control.

Internally Displaced Persons

The government considers Greek Cypriots displaced as a result of the 1974 division of the island to be refugees, although they fall under the UN definition of IDPs. As of October 2015, these individuals and their descendants numbered 226,787. UNHCR did not provide assistance to Cyprus IDPs and officially considered the IDP population to be zero. Depending on their income, IDPs were eligible for financial assistance from the government. They were resettled; had access to humanitarian organizations; and were not subject to attack, targeting, or mandatory return under dangerous conditions. Greek Cypriots and Turkish

Cypriots were engaged in ongoing UN-facilitated peace talks, including discussions to resolve the issue of their lost property.

Protection of Refugees

<u>Access to Asylum</u>: The law provides for the granting of asylum or refugee status, and the government has established a system for providing protection to refugees.

Several NGOs reported prolonged detention of detainees awaiting an asylum determination, most beyond the six months established under government policy and, in a few cases, beyond the maximum of 18 months permitted by law. Unlike in previous years, the ombudsman reported that the examination of applications of Syrian nationals seeking international protection was taking place within a reasonable timeframe.

In April three detainees at Mennoyia Detention Center for undocumented migrants climbed on the roof of the building to protest the length of their detention.

In a March 31 report based on a December 2015 visit to the country's only reception center for asylum seekers in Kofinou, the Council of Europe's commissioner for human rights deplored a 2014 law restricting the right of refugees and beneficiaries of subsidiary protection to family reunification. The commissioner welcomed the termination of the practice of detaining Syrian asylum seekers and the reduction of the capacity of Mennoyia detention center by half but noted with concern the widespread lengthy detention of failed asylum seekers and other migrants.

The government provides a special temporary "humanitarian" residency status for citizens or residents of Syria who enter the country legally or illegally. All persons seeking such status were required to provide a Syrian passport or other identification. The Ministry of Interior stated that such status was for Syrians who did not wish to apply for international protection. From January to August, authorities granted refugee status to 21 Syrians and subsidiary protection status to an additional 725. Overall, from January to October, the government granted refugee status to 187 persons.

The government funded a Greek language program for refugees, asylum seekers, unaccompanied minors, and other migrant groups. It funded five municipalities to implement integration programs for the same groups and established a reception center for unaccompanied minors. It also funded a national television station to produce a cooking show featuring traditional dishes from migrants' countries of origin.

<u>Refoulement</u>: The ombudsman and NGOs reported that asylum seekers with denied applications for asylum were deported before final adjudication of their cases. The ombudsman examined complaints from asylum seekers who were arrested for deportation while the court case challenging the rejection of their asylum applications was still pending and, in some cases, her office intervened and prevented deportations. The ombudsman warned authorities in writing that deportation in those cases could amount to an infringement of the principle of nonrefoulement.

In May 2015 the UN Committee against Torture reportedly raised concerns about reports that asylum seekers were deported to their countries of origin despite facing a serious risk of torture or religious persecution. According to the report, the committee also criticized that authorities did not protect asylum seekers from refoulement during the judicial review process and that there was no effective judicial remedy to challenge deportation decisions and halt deportations pending the outcome of appeals.

The NGO KISA visited the Mennoyia Detention Center several times during the year and reconfirmed the ombudsman's findings that detention facilities for rejected asylum seekers did not respect their fundamental rights. KISA agreed that conditions at the center had improved after the change of management, but the change did not entirely end the inhuman and degrading treatment of detainees.

<u>Employment</u>: Authorities allowed asylum seekers whose cases were awaiting adjudication to work after residing six months in the country but limited them to the areas permitted by law. The law restricts asylum seekers' employment to work in fisheries, the production of animal feed, waste management, gas stations and car washes, freight handling in the wholesale trade, building and outdoor cleaning, distribution of advertising and informational materials, and food delivery. Two NGOs claimed, however, that the Labor Department continued to refuse to approve and renew labor contracts for asylum seekers outside the farming and agriculture sector. Recognized refugees and persons with subsidiary protection have the same rights as citizens with regard to employment.

Various NGOs confirmed that residency permits contingent upon employment were virtually unobtainable, given the weak economy and the limited types of work authorized by the Labor Department. There were also reports of racism by

Labor Department officers who met with valid residency applicants seeking a contract of employment. From January to September, the Ministry of Labor and Social Insurance approved 10 labor contracts for asylum seekers, of which six were in agriculture and four in gas stations.

NGOs complained about the remoteness of the government's reception center for asylum seekers at Kofinou, the lack of language or job training, and the shortage of job opportunities other than as day laborers at nearby farms.

Access to Basic Services: Asylum seekers who refused an available job could be denied state benefits. To obtain welfare benefits, asylum seekers also needed a valid address, which was not possible for those who were homeless. NGOs and asylum seekers reported delays and inconsistencies in the delivery of benefits to eligible asylum seekers.

In July the ombudsman issued a report highlighting the problem of retroactive welfare benefits owed to asylum seekers. The ombudsman also reported that the system of providing welfare support to asylum seekers via coupons was problematic in that the special needs of vulnerable groups among asylum seekers were not taken into account or accommodated appropriately. The coupons could be redeemed only in specific shops that may lack some supplies and were usually more expensive than other grocery stores.

In contrast with 2015, there were no reports from NGOs that authorities discriminated against asylum seekers in the provision of state medical care.

Temporary Protection: The government also provided temporary protection to individuals who may not qualify as refugees. Authorities granted subsidiary protection to 946 persons in the first eight months the year.

Section 3. Freedom to Participate in the Political Process

The law and constitution provide citizens the ability to choose their government in free and fair periodic elections held by secret ballot and based on universal and equal suffrage. In national elections, only Turkish Cypriots who resided permanently in the government-controlled area were permitted to vote and run for office. In elections for the European Parliament, Cypriot citizens, resident EU citizens, and Turkish Cypriots who live in the area administered by the Turkish Cypriots have the right to vote and run for office.

Elections and Political Participation

Recent Elections: In May the country held free and fair elections for the 56 seats assigned to Greek Cypriots in the 80-seat House of Representatives. In 2013 voters elected Nicos Anastasiades president in free and fair elections.

Participation of Women and Minorities: No laws limit the participation of women and members of minorities in the political process, and women and minorities did participate. The 24 seats assigned to Turkish Cypriots in the House of Representatives were unfilled. There was one woman in the 11-seat Council of Ministers and 10 women in the 56-seat House of Representatives.

In 2014 some Turkish Cypriots complained that problems in the electoral roll disenfranchised a number of Turkish Cypriot voters. A law enacted in 2014 automatically registered all adult Turkish Cypriot holders of a Republic of Cyprus identity card residing in the area administered by Turkish Cypriots in the electoral roll for the European Parliament elections. Turkish Cypriots not residing in that area needed to apply for registration in the electoral roll, as did all other Cypriot citizens. The government did not automatically register an unspecified number of Turkish Cypriots residing in the north because they were incorrectly listed in the official civil registry as residents of the government-controlled area. The Ministry of Interior reported no developments on this issue as of October.

Section 4. Corruption and Lack of Transparency in Government

The law provides criminal penalties for corruption by officials, which vary depending on the charges, and the government generally implemented the laws effectively. There were numerous reports of government corruption during the year. The government generally investigated and prosecuted cases of corruption.

Corruption: During the year the government initiated several investigations against public officials on suspicion of corruption. In March authorities indicted 12 officials for receiving kickbacks, including the mayor of Larnaca and the former mayor of Paphos, who was in prison serving a six-year term on a separate corruption charge.

Financial Disclosure: The law requires the president of the republic, members of the Council of Ministers, and members of parliament to declare their income and assets. It does not require other public officials to declare their income or assets.

<u>Public Access to Information</u>: The constitution provides citizens the right to access government information, but there are no specific laws to implement the right. The law prohibits civil servants from providing access to government documents without first obtaining permission from the relevant minister.

Section 5. Governmental Attitude Regarding International and Nongovernmental Investigation of Alleged Violations of Human Rights

Domestic and international human rights groups generally operated without government restriction, investigating and publishing their findings on human rights cases. There is a government ombudsman, whose portfolio includes human rights, and a legislative Committee on Human Rights.

<u>Government Human Rights Bodies</u>: During her independent investigations, the ombudsman generally enjoyed good cooperation with other government bodies. The ombudsman's reports focused on police misconduct, treatment of patients at state hospitals, treatment of asylum seekers and foreign workers, and gender equality in the workplace. Citizens respected the Office of the Ombudsman and considered it effective.

The legislative Committee on Human Rights, which most local NGOs considered effective, consists of nine members of the House of Representatives who serve five-year terms. The committee discussed wide-ranging human rights problems, including trafficking in persons, prison conditions, and the rights of foreign workers. The executive branch did not exercise control over the committee.

Section 6. Discrimination, Societal Abuses, and Trafficking in Persons

Women

<u>Rape and Domestic Violence</u>: The law criminalizes rape, including spousal rape, with a maximum sentence of life in prison for violations. The government enforced the law effectively. Most convicted offenders received considerably less than the maximum sentence. In July the Cypriot Women's Lobby staged a demonstration outside the Supreme Court to protest the court's decision to reduce the prison sentence of two men found guilty in a rape case from 12 years to 10 years because the survivor had not been seriously injured. From January to August, there were 67 sexual assault cases and 11 rape cases reported to police.

There were reports of violence against women, including spousal abuse, and the number of cases reported increased sharply in recent years. The law establishes clear mechanisms for reporting and prosecuting family violence and provides that the testimony of minors and experts, such as psychologists, may be used as evidence to prosecute abusers. The law provides for the imprisonment of persons found guilty of abusing family members. The court can issue a same-day restraining order against suspected or convicted domestic-violence offenders. Doctors, hospital workers, and education professionals are required to report all suspected cases of domestic violence to police. Many victims refused to testify in court, however, and by law, one spouse cannot be compelled to testify against the other. Courts were obliged to drop cases of domestic violence if the spousal victim was the only witness and refused to testify. Between January and September, police responded to 424 domestic violence cases--285 against women, 99 against men, and 78 against children. Of those, 172 were investigated and 86 referred to court.

Survivors of domestic violence had two shelters, each funded primarily by the government and run by the NGO Association for the Prevention of Domestic Violence. The association reported receiving an average of 125 calls per month.

Police conducted detailed educational programs for officers on the proper handling of domestic violence, including training focused on child abuse. NGOs noted, however, that police dismissed claims of domestic abuse by foreign women and children.

Female Genital Mutilation/Cutting (FGM/C): While the practice was not a problem locally, the government received and occasionally granted asylum applications from migrant women subjected to FGM/C. It considered FGM/C grounds for granting refugee status. During the year it received 19 asylum applications from women who claimed they were subjected to FGM/C. Six women received refugee status and other applications were still under examination.

Sexual Harassment: The law prohibits sexual harassment in the workplace and provides a penalty of up to six months in prison and/or a 12,000 euro ($13,200) fine. The ombudsman and NGOs reported that authorities did not investigate sexual harassment complaints submitted by foreign domestic workers. The ombudsman was preparing a report on the government's handling of sexual harassment complaints submitted by domestic workers. The ombudsman was examining the complaint of a domestic worker that she was sexually harassed by three employers and eventually deported.

Sexual harassment was reportedly a widespread problem, although victims did not report most incidents to authorities. The ombudsman's 2014 annual report indicated that 10 percent of complaints submitted to the Equality Authority, a subsection of the ombudsman's office, concerned sexual harassment. Between January and September, the Department of Labor received nine complaints regarding sexual harassment, three from Cypriot nationals and six from foreign, non-EU nationals. Two of the complaints submitted by Cypriots were found valid and resolved by the employer, and the third was under investigation. The Department of Labor reported the six foreigners requested permission to change employer. In the process, one dropped the complaint, another did not come forward to give a statement, two cases lacked sufficient evidence to prove sexual harassment, and two cases were still under investigation. The Department of Labor investigated 10 complaints by non-EU foreign nationals in 2015 and did not find evidence of sexual harassment in any. The office of the ombudsman, in its capacity as the Equality Authority, provided training to police, social workers, health care providers, teachers, prosecutors, labor and immigration service personnel, and to journalists.

Reproductive Rights: Couples and individuals generally were able to decide freely the number, spacing, and timing of their children; manage their reproductive health; and to have access to the information and means to do so, free from discrimination, coercion, or violence.

Discrimination: The law provides for the same legal status and rights for women as for men. The law requires equal pay for equal work or work of equal value. The government generally enforced these laws. Women experienced discrimination in such areas as hiring, career advancement, conditions of employment, and pay.

Children

Birth Registration: Children derive citizenship from their parents, and there was universal registration at the time of birth.

Child Abuse: A University of Cyprus survey released in April 2015 showed that 25 percent of children experienced some form of sexual harassment or abuse. In March a ministerial committee set up in July 2015 approved a three-year national action plan to combat child abuse and sexual exploitation, and child pornography.

Between January and September, police investigated 98 cases of child abuse, 37 of which were referred for prosecution.

Early and Forced Marriage: The legal age of marriage is 18, but persons between the ages of 16 and 18 may marry, provided there are serious reasons justifying the marriage and their legal guardians provide written consent. A district court can also allow the marriage of persons between the ages of 16 and 18 if the parents unjustifiably refuse consent or in the absence of legal guardians.

Female Genital Mutilation/Cutting (FGM/C): Information provided in the women's section above.

Sexual Exploitation of Children: The law prohibits commercial sexual exploitation of children, child pornography, offering or procuring a child for prostitution, and engaging in or promoting a child in any form of sexual activity. The penalty for violations is up to 20 years in prison. Authorities enforced these laws. Possession of child pornography is a criminal offense punishable by a maximum of 10 years' imprisonment. Authorities enforced these laws. The minimum age for consensual sex is 17; sexual intercourse with a person under the age of 17 is a criminal offense. The penalty for sexual intercourse with a girl between the ages of 13 and 17 is a maximum of three years' imprisonment. The criminal penalty for sexual intercourse with a girl under 13 is up to life in prison.

International Child Abductions: The country is a party to the 1980 Hague Convention on the Civil Aspects of International Child Abduction. See the Department of State's *Annual Report on International Parental Child Abduction* at travel.state.gov/content/childabduction/en/legal/compliance.html.

Anti-Semitism

There were approximately 3,000 persons in the Jewish community, which consisted of a very small number of native Jewish Cypriots and a greater number of expatriate Israeli, British, and other Jews.

There were reports of verbal harassment of members of the Jewish community along with incidents of property damage.

Trafficking in Persons

See the Department of State's *Trafficking in Persons Report* at
www.state.gov/j/tip/rls/tiprpt/.

Persons with Disabilities

The law prohibits discrimination against persons with physical, sensory, intellectual, and mental disabilities in employment, education, air travel and other transportation, access to health care, the judicial system, or in the provision of other state services. The law provides persons with disabilities the right to participate effectively and fully in political and public life, including by exercising their right to vote and stand for election. The government generally enforced these provisions. While the law mandates universal accessibility for public buildings and tourist facilities built after 1999, government enforcement was ineffective. Older buildings frequently lacked access for persons with disabilities. No appropriate services or support existed for adults with mental disabilities who required long-term care.

Authorities made inadequate progress in increasing accessibility of persons with disabilities to buildings, information, and communications. The ombudsman's authority covers discrimination based on disabilities in both the private and public sectors. Problems facing persons with disabilities included access to natural and constructed environments, transportation, information, and communications. During the year the ombudsman examined a number of complaints related to lack of accessibility to public buildings, including government offices, police stations, and schools, as well as complaints concerning discrimination in the workplace and lack of accessibility to audiovisual programs.

The state provided facilities to enable children with disabilities to attend all levels of education. The Ministry of Education has adopted a code of good practices, prepared in collaboration with the ombudsman, regarding attendance of students with disabilities in special units of public schools. Authorities provided a personal assistant for students with disabilities attending public schools but not private ones.

During the year authorities implemented a deinstitutionalization program for persons with mental disabilities. Because there were no long-term care services or support specifically for persons with mental disabilities, many resided at the Athalassa Psychiatric Hospital; they were transferred to a community home for persons with disabilities. The ombudsman noted that she did not consider their deinstitutionalization complete because authorities had not developed a plan to prepare them to live independently outside an institution.

The Paraplegics Association reported that the government did not take measures to provide access to public beaches and public transport to wheelchair users. The association reported that some older buses as well as intercity buses and those providing transport to and from the airports were not accessible, while the newer ones had only one space for wheelchair users.

The Ministry of Labor and Social Insurance's Service for the Care and Rehabilitation of the Disabled is responsible for protecting the rights of persons with disabilities. The minister of labor and social insurance chaired the Pancyprian Council for Persons with Disabilities, which included representatives of government services, organizations representing persons with disabilities, and employer and employee organizations. Observers did not consider fines for violating the law against employment discrimination sufficient to deter employers from discriminating against persons with disabilities (see also section 7.d.).

National/Racial/Ethnic Minorities

Minority groups in the government-controlled area of Cyprus included Latins, Maronites, Armenians, and Roma. Although legally considered one of the two main communities of Cyprus, Turkish Cypriots constitute a relatively small proportion of the population in the government-controlled areas and experienced discrimination as a result of their heritage.

There were incidents of violence against Turkish Cypriots as well as some incidents of verbal abuse or discrimination against non-Greek Cypriots. On May 15, a group of 100 to 150 soccer fans, some on motorbikes, attacked a car with three Turkish Cypriot passengers on a main Nicosia street and used abusive language against them. Police opened a criminal investigation into the matter. The Turkish Cypriot passengers reported the case to police the following day. They complained police told them there was not much that could be done, since they did not take the motorbikes' license plates.

In March state broadcaster CyBC aired three times an interview with a popular Greek singer in which the guest used racist and offensive language against refugees fleeing to the EU, particularly Muslim refugees. In June the Radio and Television Authority ordered CyBC to pay a 26,000 euro ($29,000) fine for airing a program that incited hate.

The Task Force on School Violence--a multidisciplinary team of experts that provided immediate support and guidance to schools facing violence, youth delinquency, and incidents of racism--reported that in 2015 it provided its services responding to 185 requests from primary and secondary schools and promoted prevention programs in 30 percent of schools over the previous two years. The Ministry of Education applied a code of conduct against racism in schools that provided schools and teachers with a detailed plan on handling, preventing, and reporting racist incidents. The Ministry of Education set as one of its top three priorities for the 2015-17 school years the increase of awareness against racism and intolerance and promotion of equality and respect at all three levels of education.

The *2014 EU Roma Health Report* noted that the Romani population faced difficulties in housing, education, and employment. Roma residing in the government-controlled areas lived either in abandoned Turkish Cypriot houses or in free prefabricated houses that the government provided and maintained. These accommodations had basic facilities, such as water, electricity, sewage systems, and solar heaters, but the houses were in isolated areas, primarily to satisfy the residents of local communities who treated Roma with hostility and did not wish to live close to them. The report stated that Roma faced extreme poverty, exclusion, and hostility from the host population and suspicion and intolerance from authorities. Roma had suboptimal opportunities for employment. The main barrier was language, because many Roma did not speak either Greek or English, although the government provided Greek lessons free of charge to all citizens.

In March 2015 the Council of Europe's Advisory Committee on the Framework Convention for the Protection of Minorities issued its opinion based on findings from a December 2014 visit to the country. The committee noted incidents of racial prejudice against Romani and migrant children in schools and of Greek Cypriot parents removing their children from certain schools where there were a large number of non-Greek Cypriot students. Romani children continued to face problems, such as irregular school attendance, early dropouts, overall low academic achievement, and small number of children continuing to secondary education. The committee tied academic underachievement to weak command of the Greek language and noted that more targeted assistance was necessary to strengthen their Greek language skills. It also noted that, while two Turkish-speaking teachers were teaching Turkish language and history in the Ayios Antonios elementary school where the majority of students were Roma, no specific education material for Romani students was provided, an omission that hindered the education experience.

The Ministry of Education reported that it has continued its systematic efforts to locate and enroll Romani children in the schools nearest to their homes but had limited success in ensuring their continued school attendance due to their families' frequent movement to and from Turkish Cypriot-administered areas. The majority of Romani children were enrolled in the Ayios Antonios Primary School in Limassol, which continued to be in a priority educational zone. Since January the school has been included in an EU-funded project to provide a variety of learning opportunities for pupils and teachers. The ministry provided bilingual Turkish/Greek-speaking teachers to facilitate communication between teachers, students, and parents; provided support to students from state psychologists and the social welfare services, organized seminars for parents and legal guardians to help them integrate into the local communities; and adjusted the educational program of Romani pupils to meet their needs. It also introduced projects and activities in cooperation with NGOs to promote diversity and to engage both students and parents. The Ministry of Education's adult education centers continued to provide free lessons on the language, history, and cultural heritage of the Romani community.

Some Turkish Cypriots living in the government-controlled area reportedly faced difficulties obtaining identification cards and other government documents, particularly if they were born after 1974.

During the year the ombudsman received a complaint by a Turkish Cypriot that police subjected him to discriminatory treatment at one of the crossing points while he was crossing from the government-controlled to the Turkish Cypriot-controlled area.

The ombudsman received and examined a complaint against the state scholarship foundation that papers announcing scholarships and application forms were available only in Greek. The foundation took action to ensure scholarship documents were available in all three official languages.

The ombudsman continued to receive complaints that the government delayed approval of citizenship to children of Turkish Cypriots married to Turkish citizens who resided in the area administered by Turkish Cypriots. Instead of granting citizenship automatically to such children, the Ministry of Interior routinely sought approval from the Council of Ministers before confirming their citizenship. From January to October, the Council of Ministers did not issue any decisions granting citizenship in such cases. The Ombudsman's Office had no authority to examine the complaints because the Council of Ministers' decision to apply different criteria for granting citizenship to children born to one Turkish parent was political. It examined the cause of the delay, however, and concluded that it stemmed from delays in the Civil Registry Department's processing of applications and by the department's failure to inform the applicants about the status of their applications. Authorities automatically granted citizenship to children of Turkish Cypriots who married Turkish citizens while living outside the country.

Acts of Violence, Discrimination, and Other Abuses Based on Sexual Orientation and Gender Identity

Antidiscrimination laws exist and prohibit direct or indirect discrimination based on sexual orientation or gender identity. Antidiscrimination laws cover employment and the following activities in the public and private domain: social protection, social insurance, social benefits, health care, education, participation in unions and professional organizations, and access to goods and services. While the law provides for same-sex civil unions, LGBTI rights activists noted that the law does not prohibit "normalizing" surgeries on intersex infants, grant legal recognition to transgender individuals, or give same-sex couples the right to adopt children. NGOs dealing with LGBTI matters claimed that housing benefits favored "traditional" families. Hate crime legislation criminalizes incitement to hatred or violence based on sexual orientation or gender identity.

Despite legal protections, LGBTI individuals faced significant societal discrimination. LGBTI persons were not open about their sexual orientation or gender identity, nor did they report homophobic violence or discrimination. There were reports of employment discrimination against LGBTI applicants (see section 7.d.).

The Ministry of Education developed a code of conduct against racism and a guide for managing and recording racist incidents, which was implemented in 73 schools during the 2015-16 school year. The code addresses homophobia and transphobia.

HIV and AIDS Social Stigma

In 2015 the president of the HIV-Positive Persons Support Center stated that HIV-positive persons faced prejudice from society and their own families, largely due to lack of public awareness. She also claimed that raising public awareness on this problem was low in the government's priorities.

Promotion of Acts of Discrimination

Government-approved textbooks used at primary and secondary schools included language that was biased against Turkish Cypriots and Turks or refrained from mentioning the Turkish Cypriot community altogether. In addition, there were anecdotal reports of teachers using handouts or leading classroom discussions that included inflammatory language against Turkish Cypriots and Turks.

Section 7. Worker Rights

a. Freedom of Association and the Right to Collective Bargaining

The law, including supporting statutes and regulations, provides for the right of workers to form and join independent unions, strike, and bargain collectively with employers. Antiunion discrimination is illegal. Dismissal for union activity is illegal with reinstatement, a fine, compensation options, or all three, if the courts find the dismissal illegal. The law excludes essential services personnel from joining unions and striking. Police officers could form associations that had the right to bargain collectively.

Authorities have the power to curtail strikes in essential services defined by the law as the armed forces, police, and gendarmerie. An agreement between the government and essential services personnel provides for dispute resolution and protects workers in the sector.

The government generally enforced applicable laws. Resources and investigations were adequate in the formal sector. Penalties require payment of pecuniary damages and compensation, but unions did not consider them sufficient to deter violations. Administrative procedures were efficient and immediate, but judicial procedures were subject to delays due to a backlog.

The law provides for freedom of association and collective bargaining. The government generally protected the right of unions to conduct their activities without interference, and employers generally respected the right of workers to form and join independent unions and to bargain collectively. Although collective agreements are not legally binding, employers and employees effectively observed their terms. Workers covered by such agreements were predominantly in the larger sectors of the economy, including construction, tourism, the health industry, and manufacturing.

Private sector employers were able to inhibit union activity because of sporadic enforcement of labor regulations prohibiting antiunion discrimination, and the implicit threat of arbitrary dismissal for union activities.

b. Prohibition of Forced or Compulsory Labor

The law prohibits all forms of forced or compulsory labor, but forced labor occurred. The government did not effectively enforce the law. Inspections of the agricultural and domestic service sectors remained inadequate, and resources at the Department of Labor Inspections within the Ministry of Labor were insufficient. The maximum penalty is six years' imprisonment for forced labor of adults and 10 years' imprisonment for forced labor of minors, but actual penalties imposed were not sufficient to deter violations.

Forced labor occurred primarily in the agriculture sector. Police investigated cases of forced labor among men and women working on farms. Foreign migrant workers, children, and asylum seekers were particularly vulnerable. Employers forced foreign workers, primarily from Eastern Europe and East and South Asia, to work up to 15 hours a day, seven days a week, for very low wages and in unsuitable living conditions. In 2015 police identified more than 25 victims of labor trafficking. Employers often retained a portion of foreign workers' salaries as payment for accommodations. There have been isolated cases of Romani parents forcing their children to beg.

Also see the Department of State's *Trafficking in Persons Report* at www.state.gov/j/tip/rls/tiprpt/.

c. Prohibition of Child Labor and Minimum Age for Employment

The law prohibits the employment of children, defined as persons under the age of 15, except in specified circumstances, such as combined work-training programs for children who are at least 14 or employment in cultural, artistic, sports, or advertising activities, subject to rules limiting work hours. The law prohibits night work and street trading by children. The law also permits the employment of adolescents, defined as persons between the ages of 15 and 18, provided it is not harmful, damaging, or dangerous and subject to rules limiting hours of employment. The law prohibits employment of adolescents between midnight and 4 a.m. The minimum age for employment in industrial work is 16.

The government effectively enforced laws and policies to protect children from exploitation in the workplace. Ministry of Labor and Social Insurance inspectors were responsible for enforcing child labor laws and did so effectively. The Social Welfare Services Department of the ministry and the commissioner for the rights of the child could also investigate suspected cases of exploitation of children at work. Employment of children in violation of the law is punishable with up to two years' imprisonment, a fine of up to 17,000 euros ($18,700), or both, which were sufficient to deter violations. There were isolated examples of children under the age of 16 working for family businesses.

d. Discrimination with Respect to Employment and Occupation

Laws and regulations prohibit direct or indirect discrimination with respect to employment or occupation on the basis of race, national origin or citizenship, sex, religion, political opinion, gender, age, disability, and sexual orientation. The government did not effectively enforce these laws or regulations. Discrimination in employment and occupation occurred with respect to race, gender, disability, sexual orientation, and HIV-positive status. Violations were punishable with up to six months' imprisonment and/or up to 12,000 euros ($13,200) fine or both.

Despite a strong legal framework, the Ministry of Labor and Social Insurance's enforcement of the law governing employment and labor matters with respect to women was ineffective. Eurostat data released in May indicated that the average pay gap between men and women for equal work in the private sector was 23.9 percent in 2014 and 0.2 percent in the public sector. The ombudsman reported receiving a large number of cases of gender discrimination in the workplace, particularly against pregnant women, who were not promoted or were dismissed from employment. During the year the Ministry of Labor conducted a campaign aimed at eliminating discrimination in employment, informing the public and businesses about existing legislation. The government amended the maternity law to provide additional maternity leave in cases of multiple births, by increasing the leave by four weeks for each additional child.

A survey published in the International Journal of Manpower in 2014 suggested that LGBTI job applicants faced significant bias compared with heterosexual applicants. The survey found that gay male applicants who made their sexual orientation clear on their job application were 39 percent less likely to get a job interview than equivalent male applicants who did not identify themselves as gay. Employers were 42.7 percent less likely to grant a job interview to openly lesbian applicants than to equivalent heterosexual female applicants.

Discrimination against Romani migrant workers occurred. Turkish Cypriots faced social and employment discrimination (see section 6).

e. Acceptable Conditions of Work

Although there is no national minimum wage, there is a minimum wage for groups deemed vulnerable to exploitation. The minimum wage for shop assistants, clerks, assistant baby and child minders, health care workers, security guards, cleaners of business/corporate premises, and nursery assistants was 870 euros ($960) per month for the first six months and 924 euros ($1,020) per month thereafter. For unskilled workers in the agricultural sector, the minimum monthly wage was 455 euros ($500) with accommodation and food provided. The government set minimum salaries for non-EU nationals working as domestic workers and as cabaret performers. The minimum starting salary for live-in housekeepers was 460 euros ($510) per month. The employers covered accommodation, food, medical insurance (shared equally with the employee), visa fees, travel, and repatriation expenses. Cabaret performers' contracts typically stipulated that they receive at least 205 euros ($230) per week for 36 hours of work. Minimum salaries in these sectors are the same for local and foreign workers.

The official poverty income level is set at 60 percent of the national median equalized disposable income, as per the EU commonly agreed definition. In 2013 (the latest estimate available) the official poverty income level was 10,324 euros ($11,400) per year for a single person.

Collective bargaining agreements covered workers in almost all other occupations, including unskilled labor. The wages set in these agreements were significantly higher than the minimum wage for specific occupations.

Foreign workers were able to claim pensions, and some bilateral agreements allowed workers to claim credit in their home countries. The Migration Service was responsible for enforcing the minimum wage for foreign workers but did not actively do so.

The legal maximum workweek is 48 hours, including overtime. The law does not require premium pay for overtime or mandatory rest periods. The law stipulates that foreign and local workers receive equal treatment. The Department of Labor Relations within the Ministry of Labor and Social Insurance is responsible for enforcing these laws. Labor unions, however, reported enforcement problems in sectors not covered by collective agreements. They also reported that certain employers, mainly in the construction industry, exploited undocumented foreign workers by paying them very low wages. The penalty for violating the law on the maximum workweek is up to one year in prison, a fine up to 3,417 euros ($3,760), or both. The penalty for violating the law on the protection of wages is six months' imprisonment or a fine of up to 15,000 euros or both. The court may order the employer to pay the employee back wages.

The law protects foreign domestic workers who file a complaint with the Ministry of Labor and Social Insurance from deportation until their cases have been adjudicated. The Department of Labor Relations reported it received 888 complaints from migrant workers against their employers, of which 745 were submitted by domestic workers. The department examined 558 of the complaints. Of those, 320 were resolved by both sides signing a release agreement giving the worker the opportunity to seek employment with another employer, while 31 cases were resolved with the voluntary return of the worker to the employer on mutually agreed terms. In 23 cases, the workers chose to return home. A total of 184 cases were sent to the Ministry of Interior for final adjudication. The ministry offered 104 workers the opportunity to seek another employer; it did not renew the work permits of the remaining 80.

NGOs reported many foreign domestic workers remained reluctant to report contract violations by their employers due to fear of losing their jobs and, consequently, their work and residency permits. The ombudsman and NGOs reported ineffective investigation of sexual harassment, violence, and the mismanagement of complaints submitted by domestic workers to the Department of Labor discouraged domestic workers from submitting complaints. They reported authorities treated sexual harassment complaints by foreign domestic workers merely as requests for a change of employer. The victims were allowed routinely to change employers, but sexual harassment complaints rarely were examined.

The Department of Labor Inspection in the Ministry of Labor and Social Insurance is responsible for enforcing health and safety laws. Authorities enforced health and safety laws satisfactorily in the formal sector but not in the informal sector. Labor unions stated that more work was required to protect undocumented workers. The penalty for failing to comply with work safety and health laws was up to four years' imprisonment, a fine not to exceed 80,000 euros ($88,000), or both. From January to June, authorities prosecuted 10 persons for violations.

The Department of Labor Inspection employed 20 full-time inspectors to enforce health and safety laws. The Department of Labor Relations, on the other hand, carried out its own inspections to ensure that employers abide by other labor laws. Inspectors were not allowed to inspect private households where persons were employed as domestic workers without a court warrant.

From January to June, three persons died in work-related accidents. Workers have the right to remove themselves from situations that endanger health or safety without jeopardy to their employment, but authorities did not effectively protect employees in this situation.

THE AREA ADMINISTERED BY TURKISH CYPRIOTS

EXECUTIVE SUMMARY

Since 1974 the northern area of Cyprus has been administered by Turkish Cypriots, who in 1983 declared the northern area the "Turkish Republic of Northern Cyprus" ("TRNC"). The United States does not recognize the "TRNC," nor does any country other than Turkey. Mustafa Akinci was elected "president" in 2015 in free and fair elections. The "TRNC constitution" is the basis for the "laws" that govern the area administered by Turkish Cypriot authorities. Police and "Turkish Cypriot security forces" were ultimately under the operational command of the Turkish military, per transitional article 10 of the "TRNC constitution," which cedes responsibility for public security and defense "temporarily" to Turkey.

Authorities maintained effective control over the security forces.

The most significant problems reported during the year included domestic violence against women, limited access to some places of worship, and trafficking in persons.

Other reported problems included overcrowding in prisons and poor prison conditions; lack of separation of incarcerated adults and juveniles; societal discrimination against lesbian, gay, bisexual, transgender, and intersex (LGBTI) persons; absence of a system to handle asylum applications or protect the rights of asylum seekers; vandalism and removal of religious icons from vacant places of worship, including some sites that were damaged, close to collapse, or had been converted to other uses; corruption and cronyism in the executive and legislative branches; restrictions on freedom of speech and expression; and failure of authorities to introduce and enforce adequate labor health and safety standards.

Authorities took steps to investigate police officials following press allegations of abuses and corrupt practices. There was evidence, however, that officials sometimes engaged in corrupt practices with impunity.

Section 1. Respect for the Integrity of the Person, Including Freedom from:

a. Arbitrary Deprivation of Life and other Unlawful or Politically Motivated Killings

There were no reports that authorities or their agents committed arbitrary, unlawful or politically motivated killings.

b. Disappearance

There were no reports of politically motivated disappearances.

c. Torture and Other Cruel, Inhuman, or Degrading Treatment or Punishment

The "law" prohibits such practices, but there were reports during the year that police abused detainees. The "law" does not refer to torture, which falls under the section of the criminal code that deals with assault, violence, and battery.

The "Attorney General's Office" reported it received only one complaint during the year concerning police battery and use of force. In August the "Attorney General's Office" opened an investigation against the police officer on assault and battery charges, and a "court" case was pending against the officer who allegedly beat a 67-year-old man arrested for the sexual assault of a mentally disabled 19-year-old boy. According to reports, without informing him of the nature of his arrest, police detained, beat, and insulted the man in an effort to obtain his confession. When police later brought the victim to face and identify the alleged attacker, police discovered they had confused names with someone else. Political party leaders called for an investigation. The "Attorney General's Office" received a complaint, and an investigation was ongoing.

Prison and Detention Center Conditions

Prison and detention center conditions did not meet international standards in a number of areas, and prison overcrowding was a particular problem. Insufficient prison infrastructure, guards, and other staff were also problems.

<u>Physical Conditions</u>: The area's prison, located in the northern part of Nicosia, has a stated capacity of 294. As of October, it held 386 prisoners and pretrial detainees. Approximately 35 percent of the prison population consisted of persons awaiting trial. As of October, the prison system held 22 female prisoners, of which nine were pretrial detainees, and one juvenile. The prison did not separate adults and juveniles, and there were no detention or correction centers for children. Due to lack of space, detainees and prisoners were kept in the same cells.

In a March interview with the *Havadis* newspaper, prison director Metin Bilmem reported prison policy did not allow staff to separate the seven 14- to 17-year-old children and the twenty 19- to 20-year-old teenagers at the prison from other inmates. The article reported that the absence of a rehabilitation center at the prison and the lack of separation between juveniles and more serious offenders were helping turn younger inmates into "crime machines." The press also reported young drug users returned to prison, but as drug dealers, illustrating a claim that incarceration of young offenders with older, more serious criminals, negatively affected them once they were released.

As of August, there were no reports of deaths in the prison or detention centers during the year.

An NGO representative stated that prison facilities lacked health and other services and inmates had limited access to washing water and hot water. Human rights advocates reported the prison had an inadequate level of health care and a lack of medical supplies; no full-time doctor, psychiatrist, or psychologist; and an insufficient number of social workers. Human rights activists also reported major problems in security, including a lack of measures to reduce violence between inmates and detainees and overcrowded cells. Authorities reported a doctor visited the prison twice a week and remained on call for any emergencies. Authorities also reported potable water was provided to inmates and detainees. In September a local newspaper reported inmates were under serious risk of contracting contagious diseases at the Central Prison, including HIV, hepatitis B, and hepatitis C.

In February the Guards Association complained to *Kibris* about poor working conditions at the Central Prison. According to *Kibris*, the association asserted that the infrastructure of the prison had deteriorated, and there was a need for a new building. The association also noted that criminals who had committed minor crimes were placed near those convicted of serious crimes. It asserted conditions were such that the prison could no longer carry out its duties to protect, monitor, educate, and rehabilitate inmates and help them reenter the community.

In an April letter to *Halkinsesi*, inmates at the Central Prison announced they had started a hunger strike to protest poor prison conditions. According to the letter, inmates reported the prison was overcrowded, with more than 400 inmates housed in a facility that had a capacity of 180. Inmates also reported there were 45 persons in one cell that had capacity for only 20 and had just one shower. The inmates demanded the return of the general "amnesty law" and criticized the prison administration for not keeping its promises regarding probation. The inmates asserted that for the past 25 years there had not been any amnesties at the Central Prison.

Administration: Recordkeeping on inmates was inadequate. Community service was not available as an alternative to prison confinement for nonviolent offenders, although there were other alternatives, including warnings, conditional and unconditional release, bail, and psychological and social counseling. The scope of the "ombudsman's" duties does not include advocating for reduced or alternative sentences, addressing the status of juvenile prisoners, or improving detention or bail conditions.

Independent Monitoring: Authorities permitted prison monitoring.

d. Arbitrary Arrest or Detention

The "law" prohibits arbitrary arrest and detention, and authorities generally observed these prohibitions.

Role of the Police and Security Apparatus

Police are responsible for enforcement of the "law." The "chief of police" reports to a "general," who is nominally under the supervision of the "Prime Ministry," which holds the "security portfolio." Police and Turkish Cypriot security forces are ultimately under the operational command of the Turkish armed forces, as provided by the "TRNC constitution," which "temporarily" cedes responsibility for public security and defense to Turkey. Security forces generally cooperated with civilian authorities and were effective in enforcing the "law."

The "Attorney General's Office" continued to work with police inspection division (or occasionally the criminal investigative division) to investigate allegations of police misconduct.

Arrest Procedures and Treatment of Detainees

Judicially issued warrants are required for arrests. Authorities may not detain a person longer than 24 hours without referring the case to the "courts" for a longer period of detention. Authorities generally respected this right and usually informed detainees promptly of charges against them, although they often held individuals believed to have committed a violent offense for longer periods without charge. According to the "law," police must bring a detained person before a "judge" within 24 hours of arrest. Police can then keep the detainee in custody for up to three months, but a "judge" must review the detention after the third day and every eight days thereafter. Bail may be granted and was routinely used. There were no alternatives to bail, which is determined by the "court." Detainees' passports were confiscated by the "court," pending trial. Authorities usually allowed detainees prompt access to family members and a lawyer of their choice. Authorities provided lawyers to the indigent only for cases involving violent offenses.

Police sometimes did not observe legal protections, particularly at the time of arrest. In contradiction to the "law," some "courts" did not permit suspects to have their lawyers present when giving testimony. Suspects who demanded the presence of a lawyer were sometimes physically intimidated or threatened with stiffer charges.

<u>Detainee's Ability to Challenge Lawfulness of Detention before a Court</u>: Persons who are arrested or detained, regardless of whether on criminal or other grounds, are entitled to challenge in court the legal basis or arbitrary nature of their detention and can obtain prompt release and compensation if found to have been unlawfully detained.

e. Denial of Fair Public Trial

The "law" provides for an independent judiciary, and authorities generally respected judicial independence.

Most criminal and civil cases begin in district "courts," from which appeals are made to the "Supreme Court." There were no special "courts" for political offenses. Civilian "courts" have jurisdiction in cases where civilians face charges of violating military restrictions, such as filming or photographing military zones.

Trial Procedures

The "law" provides for the right to a fair public trial, and independent judicial authorities generally enforced this right. The "TRNC Constitution" provides for public trials, the defendant's right to be present at those trials, and the defendant's right to consult with an attorney in a timely manner. Authorities provide lawyers to indigent defendants only in cases involving violent offenses. Defendants may question witnesses against them and present evidence and witnesses on their behalf. The "law" also requires that defendants and their attorneys have access to evidence held by the "government" related to their cases. Defendants enjoy a presumption of innocence and have a right to appeal. Authorities generally respected these rights and generally respected "court" orders.

Various NGO representatives and human rights lawyers noted that defendants did not fully enjoy the right to be informed promptly and in detail of the charges brought against them. They have also noted that there was a lack of sufficient free interpretation for some languages as well as a lack of professional translation. For example, authorities recruited nonprofessional translators haphazardly, and they did not translate everything said during "court" proceedings. Insufficient translation also delayed hearings and caused longer detention periods for suspects.

Political Prisoners and Detainees

There were no reports of political prisoners or detainees.

Civil Judicial Procedures and Remedies

Individuals or organizations may seek civil remedies for human rights violations through domestic "courts." Authorities generally respect "court" orders. Individuals and organizations may appeal adverse decisions by the "courts" that involve human rights to the European Court of Human Rights (ECHR). Under ECHR rules, if adequate local remedies exist, an appellant does not have standing to bring a case before the ECHR until that appellant exhausts all local remedies.

Property Restitution

Greek Cypriots continued to pursue property suits in the ECHR against the Turkish government for the loss since 1974 of property located in the area administered by Turkish Cypriots. Turkish Cypriots pursued claims against the Republic of Cyprus as well.

In response to the ECHR's 2005 ruling in the Xenides-Arestis case that Turkey's "subordinate local authorities" in Cyprus had not provided an adequate local remedy, a property commission was established to handle claims by Greek Cypriots. In 2006 the ECHR ruled that the commission had satisfied "in principle" the ECHR's requirement for an effective local remedy. In a 2010 ruling, the ECHR recognized the property commission as a domestic remedy. As of October, claimants had filed 6,304 applications with the commission, 775 of which were concluded through friendly settlements and 25 through formal hearings. The commission has paid more than 227 million British pounds ($287 million) in compensation to applicants.

f. Arbitrary or Unlawful Interference with Privacy, Family, Home, or Correspondence

The "law" prohibits such actions. There were reports that police subjected Greek Cypriots and Maronites living in the area administered by Turkish Cypriots to surveillance. Although authorities reported otherwise, a Maronite representative asserted that during the year the Turkish armed forces occupied 18 houses in the Maronite village of Karpashia.

Section 2. Respect for Civil Liberties, Including:

a. Freedom of Speech and Press

The "law" provides for freedom of speech and press, and authorities generally respected this right. Individuals were usually able to criticize authorities publicly without reprisal, with some exceptions.

Freedom of Speech and Expression: While there is no law restricting the use of non-"TRNC" flags or symbols, some individuals who have flown Republic of Cyprus flags have been publicly criticized and put on trial on charges of "disturbing the peace" or "provocative actions."

Press and Media Freedoms: While authorities generally respected press freedom, they at times obstructed journalists in their reporting. Journalists practiced self-censorship for fear of losing their jobs in connection with investigating a story. One media representative complained that press and media representatives were prevented from getting close enough to conduct on-site reporting during incidents or to follow up reporting at "court" hearings. Journalists also alleged that owners of media outlets influenced press coverage and discouraged journalists from reporting contrary to the owners' views.

Violence and Harassment: There were reports that defendants in some "court" cases allegedly threatened journalists, who also faced pressure for their reporting from companies that advertised in their publications.

In March, three masked persons attacked a journalist departing a fitness club, inflicting head injuries that required five stitches. Police have not announced the results from their investigation of the incident.

On July 14, local newspapers reported that Mert Ozdag, a reporter, received a threatening message on his parked vehicle, which read, "Be careful. You are in trouble." Ozdag had been writing about allegations of illegal loans and illegal construction in July. Police started an investigation of the threat and were reviewing closed circuit cameras in the area. On July 15, the journalists association and NGOs condemned the threat.

Censorship or Content Restrictions: Journalists cannot access or report on persons under control of the armed forces. The Turkish Cypriot Journalists Association reported authorities used these restrictions to deny access and prevent journalists from investigating valid subjects, such as suicides or allegations of police torture or battery within the military or police systems.

Internet Freedom

Authorities did not restrict or disrupt access to the internet or censor online content, and there were no credible reports that they monitored private online communications without appropriate legal authority. Although technological developments improved the delivery methods for journalists, they reported continued difficulties in accessing public information.

In March the press reported the number of broadband users reached 68,000 in the north, including fixed line and mobile internet subscribers.

Academic Freedom and Cultural Events

Authorities did not restrict academic freedom or cultural events.

b. Freedom of Peaceful Assembly and Association

Freedom of Assembly

The "law" provides for the freedoms of assembly, and authorities usually respected this right.

The Primary Education Teachers Union reported that police prevented its members from assembling in front of the Turkish-funded Hala Sultan Religious High School in June to protest the "government's" failure to enforce the "Supreme Court's" decision that the school should operate by vocational school instead of public school regulations, thereby allowing it to separate boys and girls and require girls to wear head scarves. Two weeks later the union reported that police prevented its members from assembling in front of the Turkish "embassy" to protest the same issue.

Freedom of Association

The "law" provides for the freedom of association, and authorities generally respected this right, although some organizations faced lengthy registration processes.

c. Freedom of Religion

See the Department of State's *International Religious Freedom Report* at www.state.gov/religiousfreedomreport/.

d. Freedom of Movement, Internally Displaced Persons, Protection of Refugees, and Stateless Persons

The "law" provides for freedom of movement within the area administered by Turkish Cypriots, foreign travel, emigration, and repatriation. Authorities generally respected these rights. An intermediary NGO handled cooperation between UNHCR and Turkish Cypriot authorities. Because no "law" exists regarding the handling of asylum applications, the UNHCR representative in the Republic of Cyprus adjudicated asylum claims.

<u>Abuse of Migrants, Refugees, and Stateless Persons</u>: UNHCR reported that, with few exceptions, asylum seekers generally were treated as illegal migrants because an official framework for asylum does not exist. Most either were denied entry or deported.

<u>In-country Movement</u>: Authorities required Greek Cypriots and Turkish Cypriots to show identification cards when crossing the "Green Line." In May authorities lifted a previous requirement that Greek Cypriots and foreigners crossing into the area administered by Turkish Cypriots fill out a "visa" form.

Only Turkey recognizes travel documents issued by the "TRNC." Some Turkish Cypriots used Turkish travel documents, but many obtained travel documents issued by the Republic of Cyprus. Turkish Cypriots born after 1974 to parents who, prior to 1974, were both Republic of Cyprus citizens obtained passports relatively easily, compared with Turkish Cypriots born after 1974 to only one Cypriot parent.

Internally Displaced Persons

Turkish Cypriots considered persons displaced as a result of the island's 1974 division to be refugees, although they fell under the United Nation's definition of internally displaced persons (IDPs). At the time of the division, this number was approximately 60,000 in the north. They were resettled; had access to humanitarian organizations; and were not subject to attack, targeting, or return under dangerous conditions. Turkish Cypriots and Greek Cypriots were engaged in ongoing UN-facilitated peace talks including discussions to resolve the issues of their lost property.

Protection of Refugees

<u>Access to Asylum</u>: The 1951 Convention relating to the Status of Refugees is incorporated into Turkish Cypriot domestic "law," as were all other "laws" that originated from the British colonial period and the pre-1963 Republic of Cyprus period and were later "ratified" by the Turkish Cypriot administration. There is no "law" or system in place for dealing with asylum seekers or the protection of refugees. Turkish Cypriot authorities evaluated individuals on a case-by-case basis and generally cooperated with the UNHCR local NGO implementing partner, the Refugee Rights Association (RRA). As of October 31, the RRA reported that 279 persons claiming to be in need of international protection arrived in the Turkish Cypriot area, including at "ports of entry." As of October 31, the RRA also

directed 146 individuals either to regularize their stay in the "TRNC" or to apply for asylum in the government-controlled area with the assistance of UNHCR.

There were reports that Turkish Cypriot authorities deported numerous asylum seekers during the year before a determination was made regarding their status and that not all received facilitated access to continue their claims with UNHCR, leading to either their imprisonment or systematic deportation. Some potential asylum seekers who attempted to enter the area administered by Turkish Cypriots illegally were arrested, taken to "court," and deported after serving their sentences at the prison.

Refoulement: Authorities did not provide protection against the expulsion or return of refugees to countries where their lives or freedom would be threatened. During the year the RRA stated that, despite its efforts, authorities at ports often denied entry to asylum seekers and that those trying to enter the north illegally were usually detained and subsequently deported. As of October 31, the RRA successfully cancelled the expulsion of 64 persons, allowing them access to the territory or regularizing their stay in the "TRNC."

Human rights associations continued to work with authorities, including UNHCR, to provide protection for asylum seekers from refoulement, at times without success. With the involvement of these associations and increased facilitation from Turkish Cypriot authorities, several asylum seekers traveled to Turkey or entered the government-controlled area, through the UN-patrolled area, and started the asylum process there.

Employment: According to immigration "law," employers need official permission from the "Department of Labor" to register foreign workers. Authorities prohibited entry or deported irregular migrants without work permits. Authorities sometimes treated asylum seekers as irregular migrants and either deported them or denied them entry. In January the press reported that, as of September 2015, a total of 47,798 non-"TRNC" citizens were in possession of work permits but did not identify how many of these were asylum seekers.

A "regulation" provides that any employer of illegal workers may be fined 8,650 Turkish lira ($2,480) or face closure of their business for two months. During the year the "Labor Authority" stated that it had identified workers without work permits. As of September 30, the "Labor Authority" had checked 841 workers to verify their status and fined 134 employers of 226 illegal workers a total of 1.9 million Turkish lira ($546,000).

According to press reports, between January 1 and March 22, the Labor Authority carried out investigations at 276 workplaces and identified 102 illegal workers. The total penalties assessed were 903,600 Turkish lira ($260,000).

Access to Basic Services: According to the RRA, at the end of October, there were 73 asylum seekers residing and working (often for below-minimum wages or in exchange for food) or attending school in the area administered by Turkish Cypriots. They could not travel abroad because they would be unable to return due to their lack of status, which rendered their presence illegal according to Turkish Cypriot immigration rules. UNHCR provided financial assistance to asylum seekers only in exceptional cases.

Section 3. Freedom to Participate in the Political Process

The "law" provides Turkish Cypriots the ability to choose their "government" through free and fair periodic elections held by secret ballot and based on universal suffrage and equal suffrage.

Elections and Political Participation

Recent Elections: Turkish Cypriots choose a leader and a representative body every five years or less. In April 2015 Turkish Cypriots elected Mustafa Akinci "president" in elections that were considered free and fair. In 2013 Turkish Cypriots held early "parliamentary" elections that observers also considered free and fair.

Political Parties and Political Participation: While membership or nonmembership in the dominant party did not confer formal advantages or disadvantages, there were widespread allegations of political cronyism and nepotism.

Participation of Women and Minorities: No laws limit the participation of women and members of minorities in the political process, and women and minorities did participate.

While there were no laws or cultural practices preventing women from participating in political life, Turkish Cypriot authorities did not permit Greek Cypriots and Maronite residents to participate in Turkish Cypriot elections. The two groups were eligible to vote in Greek Cypriot elections but had to travel to the government-controlled area to exercise that right. Greek Cypriot and Maronite enclave communities in the area administered by Turkish Cypriots directly elected municipal officials. Turkish Cypriot authorities did not recognize these officials. There was no minority representation in the 50-seat "parliament" or in the "cabinet." There were four women in the 50-seat "parliament." During the year one woman was a member of the "cabinet." She has since been replaced in a new government, leaving no women in "cabinet" positions.

Section 4. Corruption and Lack of Transparency in Government

The "law" provides criminal penalties for official corruption. Authorities did not implement the "law" effectively, and "officials" sometimes engaged in corrupt practices with impunity. Observers generally perceived corruption, cronyism, and lack of transparency to be serious problems in the legislative and executive branches.

Corruption: In June the press reported that the "prime minister" used "state" funds to travel to Istanbul with a seven-person delegation to attend his daughter's graduation. The press also reported the group was given a travel advance of 5,000 Turkish lira ($1,440), reportedly paid by the "state." The same month, the People's Party (HP) filed a complaint with the "Auditor General's Office" concerning the "prime minister's" use of "state" funds to cover the delegation's travel. The HP urged that the money be returned to the "state" and an apology made to the public.

Financial Disclosure: The "law" provides that all "government" employees must declare their wealth and assets, including those who are elected; "Council of Ministers" appointees; all "judges" and "prosecutors;" the "ombudsman"; the chair of the "Attorney General's Office;" and "Attorney General's Office" members. Every five years employees who fall under this definition must declare any movable and immovable property, money, equity shares, stocks, and jewelry worth five times their monthly salary, as well as receivables and debts that belong to them, their spouses, and all children under their custody. The disclosure is made internally and is not public information. Once a declaration is overdue, the employee receives a written warning to disclose wealth within 30 days. If the disclosure is not forthcoming, a complaint is filed with the "Attorney General's Office." The penalty for noncompliance is a fine of up to 5,000 Turkish lira ($1,440) or three months' imprisonment, or both. If confidentiality is violated, employees may receive a fine of up to 10,000 Turkish lira ($2,870), 12 months' imprisonment, or both.

<u>Public Access to Information</u>: The "constitution" provides free access to "government" information, and the "law" provides for public access. "Civil servants" were not allowed to provide access to "government" documents without first obtaining permission from their superiors or "minister." NGO representatives complained that there were delays, out-of-date information, and problems concerning access. One NGO complained about the procedure of accessing information and claimed that some access was denied or deliberately delayed.

Section 5. Governmental Attitude Regarding International and Nongovernmental Investigation of Alleged Violations of Human Rights

A limited number of domestic human rights groups operated in the area administered by Turkish Cypriots. Many local human rights groups were concerned with human rights conditions in the area administered by Turkish Cypriots. NGOs promoted awareness of domestic violence; women's rights; rights of asylum seekers, refugees, and immigrants; trafficking in persons; police abuse; and the rights of LGBTI persons. These groups had little impact on specific "legislation" to improve the protection of human rights.

Section 6. Discrimination, Societal Abuses, and Trafficking in Persons

Women

<u>Rape and Domestic Violence</u>: The "law" criminalizes rape, including spousal rape, and provides for a maximum sentence of life imprisonment. Authorities and police enforced the "law" effectively. There were local NGOs whose specific mission was to support rape victims. One NGO representative reported societal pressure against reporting incidents of spousal rape.

Violence against women, including spousal abuse, remained a problem. The "law" prohibits domestic violence under a general assault/violence/battery clause in the "criminal code." While allegations of domestic violence were usually considered a family matter and settled without prosecution, a few cases of domestic violence were prosecuted and resulted in fines and bail for the perpetrator but no prison sentences.

In July the Social Risks Foundation NGO announced it was closing the only women's shelter in the north after financial problems and problems between trafficking victims and domestic violence survivors. At a press conference, the foundation stated that, over a period of five years, the house had sheltered 227 women who had been subjected to domestic violence and 114 children living with them.

The "Attorney General's Office" reported that, between January and October, 102 domestic violence complaints were made to police. Of these, 34 were referred to the "courts" and were pending trial, 18 were withdrawn after police gave warnings to the offender, 11 were resolved with the payment of fines, and 39 investigations were ongoing.

In October an NGO reported that police humiliated and neglected victims of domestic violence. The NGO also reported one of the biggest problems was women's lack of access to family courts for protection orders and other legal rights, including divorce.

Sexual Harassment: The "criminal code" prohibits sexual harassment and considers it a misdemeanor punishable by up to 12 months' imprisonment and/or an unspecified fine. According to NGOs, incidents of sexual harassment went largely unreported.

Reproductive Rights: Couples and individuals have the right to decide the number, spacing, and timing of their children; manage their reproductive health; and have access to the information and means to do so, free from discrimination, coercion, or violence.

Discrimination: The law provides for the same legal status and rights for women as for men. Women experienced discrimination in such areas as employment, credit, owning or managing businesses, education, and housing. The "government" generally enforced "laws" requiring equal pay for men and women performing the same work at the white-collar level. Women working in the agricultural and textile sectors routinely received less pay than their male counterparts.

In June the press reported that a number of NGOs criticized the Near East University Hospital for firing a woman working in the hospital after she became pregnant.

Children

Birth Registration: Children derive "citizenship" from their parents, and there was universal registration at birth, including children born to migrants.

<u>Child Abuse</u>: There were reports of child abuse. As with domestic violence, there were social and cultural disincentives to seeking legal remedies for such problems, which observers believed were underreported.

<u>Early and Forced Marriage</u>: The minimum age of marriage for girls and boys is 18. A "court" may allow marriages for minors who are between the ages of 16 and 18 if they receive parental consent.

<u>Sexual Exploitation of Children</u>: The "criminal code" prohibits commercial sexual exploitation of children, and authorities generally enforced the prohibition. The age of consent is 16. Statutory rape or attempted statutory rape of a minor under the age of 16 is classified as a felony, and the maximum penalty is life imprisonment. If the offender is under 18 and two years or less apart in age from the victim, the act is a misdemeanor punishable by up to two years in prison and/or an unspecified fine. There are no "laws" regarding child pornography.

Anti-Semitism

The small Jewish community consisted primarily of nonresident businesspersons. There were no reports of anti-Semitic acts.

In April a group of 50 Palestinian students protested and boycotted a conference presentation by an Israeli professor who was a guest speaker at the Eastern Mediterranean University (EMU). Approximately 50 Palestinian students opened banners during the conference reading, "Free Palestine," "Terrorist Israel," and held photos of suffering Palestinian children. The students did not shout or interrupt the conference but rather made their protests in silence with banners. Police and private security intervened and removed the students from the conference hall. Observers reported that there were approximately 1,000 Palestinian students studying at EMU.

Trafficking in Persons

See the Department of State's *Trafficking in Persons Report* at www.state.gov/j/tip/rls/tiprpt/.

Persons with Disabilities

The "law" prohibits discrimination against persons with physical, sensory, intellectual, and mental disabilities in employment, education, air travel and other transportation, access to health care, the "judicial system," or the provision of other "state" services, and authorities effectively enforced these provisions. The "law" does not mandate access to public buildings and other facilities for persons with disabilities, and the disability community complained of the absence of infrastructure in public areas, including lack of sidewalks, blocked sidewalks, and the inability to use public transportation.

In May the "parliament chair," Sibel Siber, established a platform for persons with disabilities so they could access the "parliament" building and observe sessions or hold meetings in their wheelchairs. In August a local municipality established a platform by the shore to allow wheelchair users to access the sea.

National/Racial/Ethnic Minorities

The "law" prohibits discrimination, and the 1975 Vienna III Agreement remains the legal source of authority regarding the treatment of the 335 Greek Cypriot and 87 Maronite residents in the area administered by Turkish Cypriots.

Under the Vienna III Agreement, the UN Peacekeeping Force in Cyprus (UNFICYP) visited enclaved Greek Cypriot residents weekly and Maronites twice a month; additional visits require preapproval by Turkish Cypriot authorities. Although the Vienna III Agreement provides for medical care by a doctor from the Greek Cypriot community, authorities permitted such care only by registered Turkish Cypriot doctors. Individuals living in enclaves also traveled to the government-controlled area for medical care.

Greek Cypriots and Maronites were able to take possession of some of their properties but were unable to leave their properties to heirs residing in the government-controlled area. A Maronite representative asserted that Maronites were not allowed to bequeath property to heirs who do not reside in the area administered by Turkish Cypriots and possess "TRNC" identification cards. Authorities allowed the enclaved residents to make improvements to their homes and apply for permission to build new structures on their properties. Maronites living in the government-controlled area could use their properties in the north only if those properties were not under the control of the Turkish military or allocated to Turkish Cypriots.

A small Kurdish minority that emigrated from Turkey in the 1980s lived in the area administered by Turkish Cypriots. There were reports of social and job discrimination against the Kurds as well as allegations that police closely monitored Kurdish activities, in particular the annual Nowruz Festival.

Authorities noted that the majority of foreign workers were from Turkey and worked in the service (hotel, restaurant, catering) and construction sectors. In August a local NGO reported on the poor working and living conditions of seasonal workers in the north. According to the NGO, workers were promised clean accommodations, but instead were housed in terrible conditions and their children often did not attend school due to proper paperwork not having been filed.

Acts of Violence, Discrimination, and Other Abuses Based on Sexual Orientation and Gender Identity

The "law" prohibits discrimination based on sexual orientation or gender identity. Homosexuality remained a social taboo and was rarely discussed. Few LGBTI persons were publicly open about their sexual orientation or gender identity.

While there were no cases recorded of official or societal discrimination based on sexual orientation in employment, housing, or access to education or health care, members of the LGBTI community noted that an overwhelming majority of LGBTI persons hid their sexual orientation or gender identity to avoid such problems.

Section 7. Worker Rights

a. Freedom of Association and the Right to Collective Bargaining

The "law" provides for the rights of workers, except members of police and Turkish Cypriot security forces, to form and join independent unions of their own choosing without prior authorization. The "law" allows all unions to conduct their activities without interference and provides for the right to strike, provided that a union notify authorities in writing if the duration of a strike was planned for longer than 24 hours. The "law" does not provide for reinstatement of workers fired for union activities nor permit "judges," members of the police force, and Turkish Cypriot security forces to strike. The "Council of Ministers" has the power to curtail a strike in any individual sector twice a year for up to 60 days if it affects the general health, security, or public order or if it prevents the provision of essential services. There is no list of what constitutes essential services. The "law" provides for collective bargaining but does not prohibit antiunion discrimination.

According to union representatives, the "government" did not effectively enforce applicable "laws." Despite having the rights of freedom of association and collective bargaining, there was very little unionization among the estimated 70,000 to 80,000 workers in the private sector. According to a union representative, if private sector workers affected business operations while seeking their rights, the employer would likely replace them. Labor authorities and the "state" did not provide adequate resources, inspections, or improvements and did not implement labor "laws." There was one labor inspector, and a written complaint from a union was required to begin an investigation. If necessary the "registrar's office" filed a complaint with the "Attorney General's Office." Any employer convicted of violating the "law" can be fined from two to eight times the monthly minimum wage of 1,834 Turkish lira ($527).

Workers formed and joined independent unions. Some companies pressured workers to join unions that the company led or approved. Officials of independent unions claimed that authorities created rival public sector unions to weaken the independent unions.

Workers exercised the right to bargain collectively. Public and semipublic employees benefited from collective bargaining agreements. Semipublic employees worked for companies run jointly by public and private enterprises where, for example, the "government" handled administration while the company's budget came from private sources.

Private sector employers were able to discourage union activity because the enforcement of labor "regulations" in the private sector was sporadic.

In March, following the death of a construction worker, unions and NGOs held a demonstration calling for mandatory unionization in the private sector.

b. Prohibition of Forced or Compulsory Labor

"Laws" prohibit all forms of forced or compulsory labor. The "government" did not effectively enforce the "law." Information regarding the adequacy of inspections and resources was not available. Forced labor was reportedly punishable by up to one year in prison, a term that was not commensurate with other serious crimes and was not adequate to deter violations. There were reports of forced labor during the year.

Conditions of forced labor existed for men and women employed in the industrial, construction, agriculture, restaurant, domestic, and retail sectors. Migrant workers in the construction and agricultural sectors were subjected to reduced wages and nonpayment of wages, beatings, and threats of deportation.

Also see the Department of State's *Trafficking in Persons Report* at www.state.gov/j/tip/rls/tiprpt/.

c. Prohibition of Child Labor and Minimum Age for Employment

The minimum age for restricted employment is 15, the last year for which education is compulsory. Employers may hire children between the ages of 15 and 18 in apprentice positions under a special status. Children over the age of 15 are restricted to not more than six hours per day and 30 hours per week. The "law" prohibits children between the ages of 15 and 18 from working during mealtimes, at night, in heavy physical labor, and under dangerous conditions. The "law" also states that every six months the employer must prove, with medical certification, that the physical work done by a child is suitable for children. Written parental consent is also required, and children are entitled to the hourly wage of a full-time employee. The "law" generally provides protection for children from exploitation in the workplace.

The "Ministry of Labor and Social Security" is responsible for enforcing child Labor "laws" and policies. Resources and inspections were not adequate to deter violations. Penalties for violations consist of fines and "court" procedures. An employer may be fined 8,650 Turkish lira ($2,480) per incident of child labor.

NGOs alleged authorities did not always effectively enforce the "laws," and employers used children, mainly from Turkey, for labor, primarily working alongside their families in the agricultural, manufacturing, automotive, and construction sectors. NGOs reported children worked in dangerous conditions, such as on construction sites, and were subjected to heavy physical work despite "legal" prohibitions. One NGO reported that some employers delayed applying for work permits for seasonal agricultural workers from Turkey, which prevented the workers' children from being eligible for local schooling.

According to one NGO, child labor in the urban informal economy was also a problem, albeit to a lesser extent than in the agricultural and manufacturing sectors. The number of children selling tissues or other small items on the street increased, particularly in neighborhoods in Nicosia with large immigrant populations. It was common in family-run shops for children to work after school and for young children to work on their family farms.

Also see the Department of Labor's *Findings on the Worst Forms of Child Labor* at www.dol.gov/ilab/reports/child-labor/findings/.

d. Discrimination with Respect to Employment and Occupation

The "law" generally prohibits discrimination with respect to employment or occupation regarding race, sex, gender, disability, language, sexual orientation and/or gender identity, and social status. The "law" does not specifically address discrimination with respect to religion, political opinion, or HIV-positive status. The "government" did not effectively enforce these "laws." Discrimination in employment and occupation occurred with respect to race, ethnicity, sex, disability, and gender.

Foreign migrant workers faced societal discrimination, with respect to ethnicity, race, and religious belief. Women were paid far less than men in the private sector, faced sexual harassment in the workplace, and held far fewer managerial positions. Greek Cypriots faced social and employment discrimination. LGBTI individuals often hid their orientation in the workplace. Disabled persons routinely found it difficult physically to access traditional workplace settings, such as office buildings.

e. Acceptable Conditions of Work

The "government" increased the minimum wage from 1,675 Turkish lira ($481) to 1,834 Turkish lira ($527), but inflation and cost of living outpaced the wage increase. Limited information was available on conditions of work. Accommodations for migrant workers, either as part of their compensation or for those made to pay, were substandard.

The standard workweek for the private and public sectors is 40 hours. There is premium pay for overtime in the public sector. Premium pay for overtime is also required, but frequently not paid, in the private sector. The "law" prohibits compulsory overtime and provides for paid annual holidays.

The "Ministry of Labor and Social Security" is responsible for enforcing both the minimum wage and paying public sector wages, but did not effectively do so. For example, in September workers for the Yenierenkoy "municipality" had not received salaries for two months. Employers paid undocumented migrant workers below the minimum wage.

Occupational safety and health standards are not current. Despite occasional inspections of working conditions by labor authorities, enforcement was rare and authorities did not effectively enforce standards in all sectors. There was little improvement in working conditions, particularly for hazardous sectors and vulnerable groups. It was common practice to deport migrant workers claiming violations. Authorities did not apply penalties to violators, and resources and inspections were not adequate to protect worker rights. The "government" has not established social protections for workers in the informal economy.

According to labor authorities, as of April, there were 41 workplace accidents, two of which resulted in fatalities. Workers could not remove themselves from situations that endangered health or safety without jeopardy to their employment. Authorities did not protect workers in these situations.